BASEBALL EXPRESSIONS & TERMINOLOGY HANDBOOK

ANDREW DINGER
ILLUSTRATED BY JESS DINGER

Baseballedgy: Baseball Expressions & Terminology Handbook
Copyright © 2020 by Andrew Dinger

Illustrations by Jess Dinger

All rights reserved. This book or any portion thereof may not be reproduced or used in any manner whatsoever without the express written permission of the publisher except for the use of brief quotations in a book review.

Ballegdy Publishing
Austin, Texas
www.Baseballedgy.com

Layout by www.formatting4U.com

ISBN 978-1-7345573-0-5

Printed in the United States of America
First Printing, 2020

I wrote Baseballedgy—Baseball Expressions & Terminology Handbook, to explain to players, parents and grandparents many fun, useful, and unique baseball terms and phrases. A lot of the terms are idioms, which means that they are completely different than what a person thinks of when they hear them. Examples are Ducks on the Pond, Frozen Rope, Rolling a Pair, and Snow Cone.

I play select/travel baseball and while I was learning the game, I was always curious about the advanced baseball terms my dad and coaches were using. I would ask my dad about them and what they meant. One day, on the way home from baseball practice, that same situation happened, and I realized that I was getting to know many terms, so I got the idea of the book. I wrote the book so that young players and their parents/grandparents could learn and understand the expressions and terms of baseball. Also, it would give young players an advantage of knowing the terms and expressions that their coaches might use with them, instead of them having to ask someone else because they didn't understand.

Baseballedgy is a fun book to read and can serve as a "go-to" reference when terms are being used. I hope that this book will be helpful to thousands of children, parents and grandparents while also providing an enjoyable reading experience to all.

Special thanks to my sister, Jess, for drawing the illustrations for the book and my parents for their support and encouragement to write the book.

                              Andrew Dinger
                              Austin, TX
                              March 2020

Table of Contents

The Field 1
Batting 9
Base Running 71
Pitching 79
Fielding 107
Index 147

The Field

Yard

Diamond

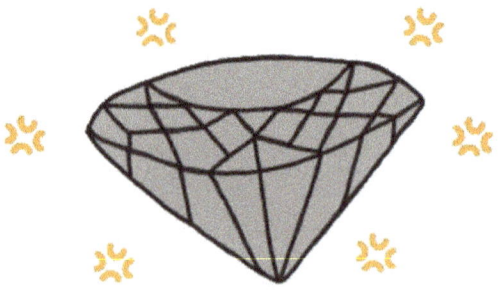

The baseball field itself is referred to as the **Yard**.

Sometimes the baseball field is called a **Diamond**, but really **Diamond** refers to the bases being in a **Diamond** shape from home plate to first base, to second base, to third base, and back to home plate.

Dugout

Bullpen

A **Dugout** is an area with a long bench where a team sits during a game. The field has two **Dugouts**, one along the first base line and the other along the third base line. Traditionally the home team sits in the third base **Dugout** and the visiting team sits in the first base **Dugout**.

A **Bullpen** is an area, outside of the field, where pitchers can warm up and practice before they go into the game. Often back-up pitchers and catchers will sit in the **Bullpen** during the game waiting to be called by the coach to warm up.

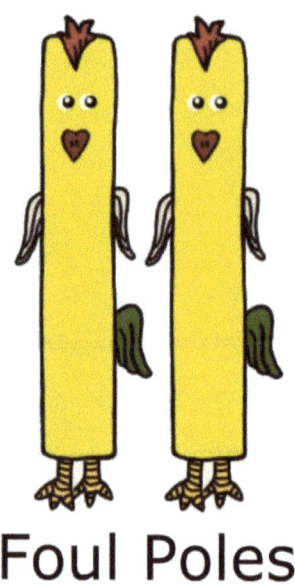

Foul Poles

Warning Track

A baseball field has two foul lines that mark the boundary of play. One foul line goes from home plate to first base and continues all the way through the outfield to the fence. The other foul line goes from home plate to third base and continues all the way through the outfield to the fence. Where the foul lines and the fences connect, there are tall yellow poles called **Foul Poles**. They are tall so that if a ball was hit past it in the air, the umpire would be able to tell whether it was a fair ball or a foul ball.

A **Warning Track** is important for player safety. **Warning Tracks** are sections of the field next to fences and walls that are different from the grass or turf (usually dirt or painted turf) that alerts players who are running toward a fence or wall, while chasing after a ball, that they are getting close to a fence or wall.

Batting

Ahead in the Count

Behind in the Count

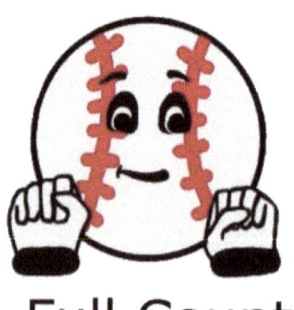

Full Count

Ahead in the Count

Behind in the Count

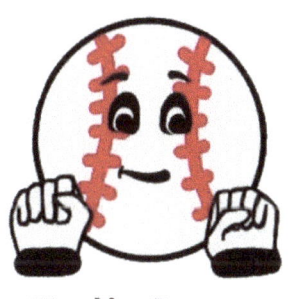

Full Count

Batting

A batter gets up to 4 balls (a walk) or 3 strikes (a strikeout) unless they hit the ball before walking or striking out. During the at-bat the umpire will keep track of how many balls and strikes the batter has, this is called the **Count**. When the umpire states what the **Count** is, they will always tell the number of balls first, then the number of strikes. For example, if the umpire says that the count is "2 and 1" that means there are 2 balls and 1 strike on the batter. Another way that the umpire indicates what the **Count** is on the batter is with their fingers. They will hold up their hands, and using their fingers, show the number of balls with their left hand and the number of strikes with their right hand.

A batter is said to be **Ahead in the Count** when there are more balls than strikes (1 and 0, 2 and 0, 3 and 0, 2 and 1, 3 and 1).

A batter is said to be **Behind in the Count** when there are more strikes than balls (0 and 1, 1 and 2, 0 and 2).

A **Full Count** is when the batter has 3 balls and 2 strikes (3 and 2). The umpire will either hold up 3 fingers in their left hand and 2 fingers in their right hand or hold up both hands with closed fists.

Plate

Batter's Box

On Deck

In The Hole

Home plate is referred to as the **Plate** or the **Dish**. When a player is at bat, they stand next to home plate in the **Batter's Box** (rectangular shaped areas on each side of home plate) while attempting to hit the ball from the pitcher. The batter must stay inside the **Batter's Box** while hitting. A player who is at bat is also referred to as being at the **Plate** or at the **Dish**.

The player who will be the next batter is said to be **On Deck**. They stand outside the **Dugout** and prepare to hit by taking some practice swings. If there is a designated spot for the **On Deck** hitter to stand, it is called the **On Deck** Circle.

A player is said to be **In the Hole** when they are the next player to be **On Deck**. They remain in the **Dugout** and gather their equipment (helmet, bat, arm/foot guard, etc.) in preparation to go to the **On Deck** circle.

The player who bats fourth in the batting order is called the **Clean Up** hitter. The **Clean Up** hitter is often one of the best batters on the team and is placed fourth in the batting order to "**Clean Up**" the bases with a big hit when the batters in front of them get on base.

Donut

Donut

The player who bats fourth in the batting order is called the **Clean Up** hitter. The **Clean Up** hitter is often one of the best batters on the team and is placed fourth in the batting order to "**Clean Up**" the bases with a big hit when the batters in front of them get on base.

A **Donut** is a weight that fits on a bat. It is usually made of plastic-coated metal. The **Donut** is put on a bat by an **On Deck** hitter who then swings the weighted bat a few times while waiting for their turn to hit. After swinging the bat with the **Donut** on it, the **Donut** is removed and then the bat feels very light and easy to swing.

Cut

Hack

When a batter swings at a pitch they are taking a **Cut** at the ball. It is also referred to as taking a **Hack** at it.

Protecting The Plate

Battling

A batter is said to be **Protecting the Plate** when they have 2 strikes on them, and they make sure that they swing at pitches that are in the **Strike Zone** or close enough to the **Strike Zone** that they could possibly be called strikes by the umpire.

Battling is when a batter has a long at bat because they are fouling off pitches that would be strikes. This extends the time they are hitting and makes the pitcher throw more pitches.

Choke Up

When a batter needs more control of their bat they will **Choke Up**, which means that they will move their hands up the bat a few inches which makes the bat shorter and lighter. A batter may **Choke Up** when they are **Protecting the Plate**.

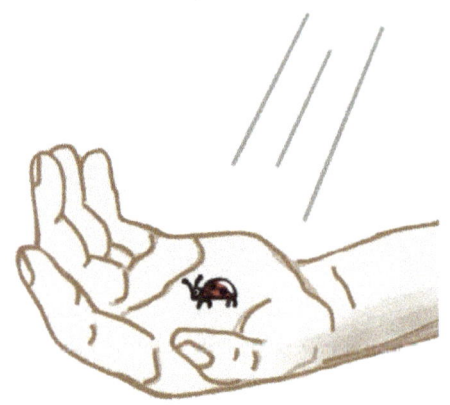

Laying It Down

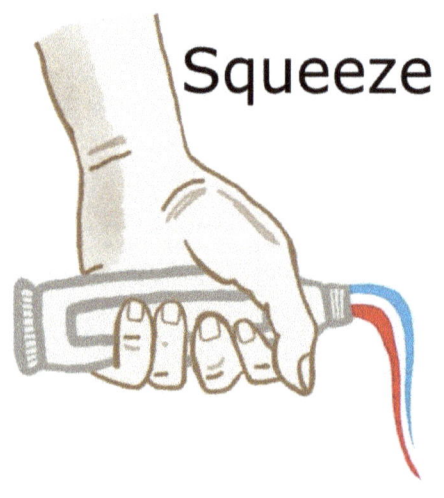

Squeeze

Laying it Down is when a batter bunts the ball. Bunting is when the batter holds their bat out and hits the pitched ball without swinging. This makes the ball go a very short distance and the infielders have to run to get the ball. Bunts are usually done to help base runners get to the next base, but sometimes a batter will surprise the fielders and bunt as a way to get on base.

A **Squeeze** play is when there is a runner on third base, and they run to home while the batter bunts the ball. There are two kinds of **Squeeze** plays, the Safety **Squeeze** and the Suicide **Squeeze**. A Safety **Squeeze** is when the runner on third base takes off for home after they see that the batter successfully bunts the ball. A Suicide **Squeeze** is when the runner on third base takes off for home as soon as the pitcher throws the pitch. The reason it is called suicide is because the runner will most likely be tagged out if the batter does not successfully bunt the ball.

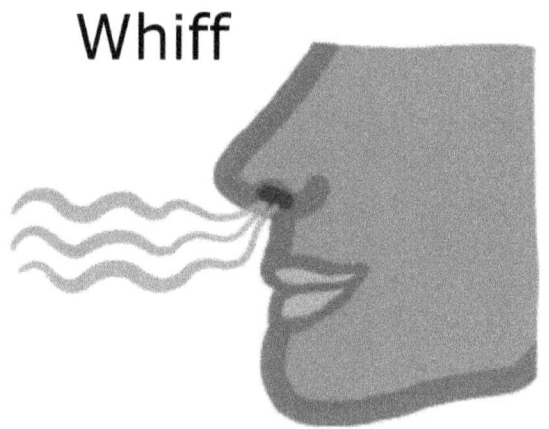

A **Whiff** is when a batter swings at a pitch but misses the ball completely.

If a batter strikes out, it is sometimes called **Whiffing**.

Caught Looking

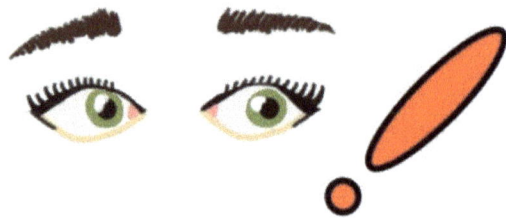

Caught Looking

A **Whiff** is when a batter swings at a pitch but misses the ball completely.

If a batter strikes out, it is sometimes called **Whiffing**.

A batter is said to be **Caught Looking** when they have 2 strikes on them and do not swing at a pitch that is called "strike 3" by the umpire. They are then out by a strikeout and were **Caught Looking**.

Stepping in the Bucket

A batter should step forward, toward the pitcher, when swinging. If a batter steps sideways (away from home plate) instead of forward, they are said to be **Stepping in the Bucket**.

Foul Ball

Getting a Piece of It

A **Foul Ball** is when a batter hits the ball, but it does not land in the field of play. The field of play is the area starting at home plate and between the right field foul line (going from home plate to first base and on to the foul pole at the outfield fence) and the left field foul line (going from home plate to third base and on to the foul pole at the outfield fence).

Getting a Piece of It is when a batter hits just enough of the ball for it to go foul (usually backwards).

Walk

Base on Balls

Wear It

A **Walk** is also called a **Base on Balls** and happens when the batter gets 4 pitches that are not strikes before they either hit the ball or strike out. When the batter gets 4 balls, they automatically get to go to first base.

Another way that a batter can get a **Walk** is if they are hit by a pitched ball. The batter's natural reaction is to get out of the way if a pitch is coming at them, but **Wear It** is when the batter allows the ball to hit them, therefore getting a **Walk** and they head to first base.

Grounder

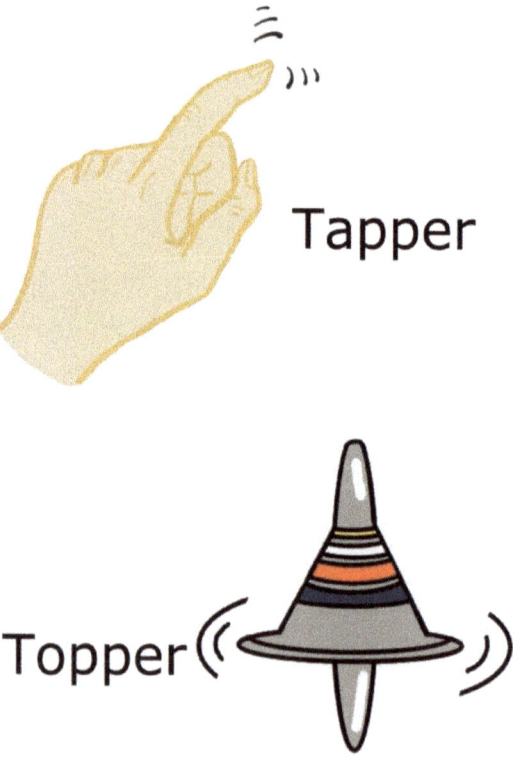
Tapper

Topper

A **Grounder** means a ball hit by a batter that goes along the ground. If it is caught by an infielder, they then attempt to throw the ball to a base to get an out. If it goes through the infield without being caught, then it is a hit for the batter.

Tapper and **Topper** are ground balls that were not hit well. **Tappers** are usually poorly hit balls that stay close to the ground. **Toppers** are usually balls that bounce because the batter hit the top of the ball and the ball went almost straight down off the bat, causing the bounces.

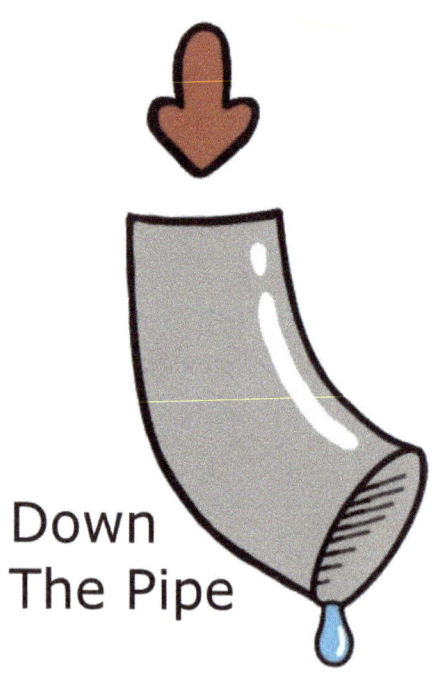

Down The Pipe

On a Platter

A batter is looking for a good pitch to hit. When they get one that is especially good it is referred to as being **Down the Pipe** or served **On a Platter**.

One Bagger

Two Bagger

Three Bagger

A **One Bagger** is when a batter gets a hit and reaches first base safely (single); a **Two Bagger** is when a batter gets a hit and reaches second base safely (double); and a **Three Bagger** is when a batter gets a hit and reaches third base safely (triple).

Rip It

Crush It

Give It A Ride

Rip It, **Crush It**, and **Give it a Ride** are all terms for a batter hitting the ball really hard. The result does not necessarily have to be a single, double, triple or home run for the batter, but just describing the way they hit the ball so well.

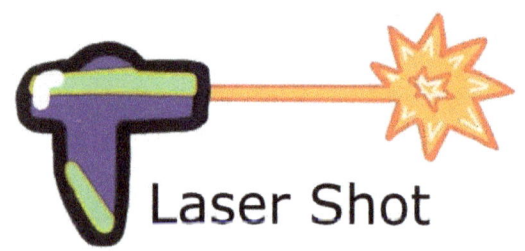

Laser Shot

Frozen Rope

Laser Shot and **Frozen Rope** are terms for hard hit line drives. A line drive is a ball hit in the air that stays low and looks like it is straight as a line. **Laser Shots** and **Frozen Ropes** refer to line drives that are hit super hard.

Wheelhouse

Power Alley

A **Wheelhouse** is where a batter's swing is the strongest. The location of the **Wheelhouse** varies from batter to batter, but usually is "belt high." When a batter gets a pitch in their **Wheelhouse**, they hit it very hard.

Power Alley refers to the area in the outfield between the outfielders. One **Power Alley** is the area between the left fielder and the center fielder, and the other **Power Alley** is between the right fielder and center fielder. When a batter hits the ball hard and it goes between the outfielders (and usually goes all the way to the fence) it is called hitting it to the **Power Alley**.

Dinger

Bomb

Jack

Moon Shot

Going Yard

Monster Shot

Dinger, **Jack**, and **Going Yard** all mean hitting the ball over the fence for a home run.

Bomb, **Moon Shot**, and **Monster Shot** are used when the batter hits a towering home run that clears the fence by a long way.

Back to Back

When two batters in a row get base hits, it is referred to as **Back to Back** hits. If the two batters get the same type of hits in a row, then it is identified with the type of hits they get, like **Back to Back** doubles.

Back to Back jacks means that the two batters hit home runs.

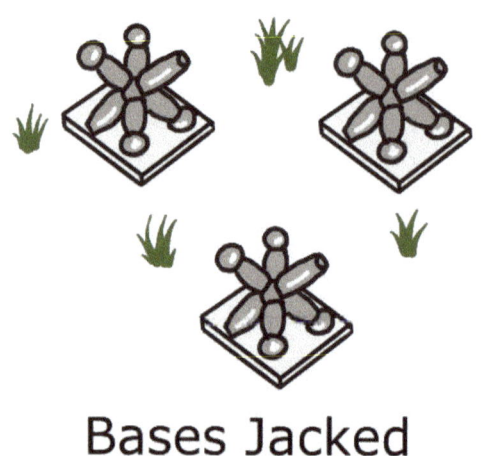

Bases Jacked

Ducks on the Pond

When the bases are loaded, it means that there are runners on all three bases. This is also referred to as having the **Bases Jacked.**

Ducks on the Pond refers to having runners on base for the batter to hit in. Often, it refers to two or more runners on base.

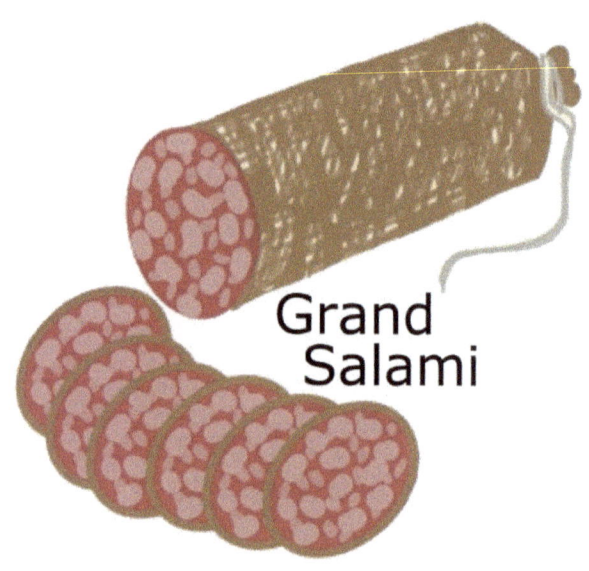

A **Pull Hitter** is a batter who almost always hits the ball to the strong side of the field. If the batter is a righthanded **Pull Hitter**, they will usually hit the ball to the left side of the field (between second base and third base). If the batter is a lefthanded **Pull Hitter**, they will usually hit the ball to the right side of the field (between second base and first base).

Good Eye

Check Swing

A batter is said to have a **Good Eye** if they know their strike zone well and don't swing at pitches that are outside of their strike zone. Coaches and fans will often yell "**Good Eye**" to a batter who resists swinging at a ball that is just outside of their strike zone.

A **Check Swing** is when a batter starts to swing at a pitch but changes their mind and stops their swing in time for it not to count as a swing. As long as the batter stops their bat before it crosses over home plate, it is considered a **Check Swing** and does not count as a swing.

Green Light

A **Green Light** is when the coach gives a batter permission to swing at the next pitch if they like it or they give a runner the choice to attempt to steal a base if they feel they can do it. For a batter, a **Green Light** is usually given on a 3 and 0 count. Normally the coach tells batters not to swing (take the pitch) when the count is 3 and 0, but a **Green Light** means to hit the pitch if the batter likes it. For a base runner, a **Green Light** is usually given to a fast runner who has good stealing skills.

Walk Off

When the home team is batting in the last inning (or in extra innings) and the batter brings home the winning run, the game ends at that point and it is referred to as a **Walk Off** victory. **Walk Off** home runs are the most exciting end to a game and are cause for great celebration!

Cycle

Hit and Run

When a player hits a single, double, triple and home run all in one game, it is called hitting a **Cycle**. The player can get the hits in any order as long as they have at least one of each type of hit during the game.

Hit and Run is when a base runner takes off like they are going to steal, and the batter hits the pitch in order to keep the runner going. Since the runner is already going, it gives them the opportunity to make it to an extra base when the ball is hit. It is important for the batter to hit a ground ball on a **Hit and Run** so the runner can keep going. If the batter hits a fly ball, the runner will have to stop running and hurry back to the base they started from.

When a team is winning in a close game and they score another run, it is called an **Insurance Run** because it gives them a better chance to protect their lead.

Base Running

Steal

Caught Stealing

A **Steal** is when a base runner runs from one base to another during a pitch. If the runner makes it to the next base without being tagged by a fielder with the ball, then the runner successfully stole the base.

Caught Stealing is when a base runner is attempting to **Steal** a base but is tagged by a fielder with the ball before reaching the base.

Tag Up

When a ball is hit up in the air by a batter (**Fly Ball**), a base runner can attempt to **Tag Up**, which means to run to the next base, but the runner cannot leave their current base until the fielder touches the fly ball. The runner usually stands with one foot on the base, ready to run, while watching the fielder to see when they touch the ball. As soon as the fielder touches it, the runner takes off for the next base.

Pickle

A base runner who ends up between two bases when the fielders have the ball is said to be in a **Pickle**. The runner who is caught in a **Pickle** goes back and forth between the two bases avoiding being tagged by a fielder with the ball. In most cases the runner gets tagged out.

A **Pickle** is also referred to as a **Rundown** or a **Hot Box**.

Pitching

Strike Zone

Paint The Corner

Framing

In order for a pitcher to throw a strike, they must throw the pitch in the batter's **Strike Zone**. The **Strike Zone** is defined as an imaginary rectangle, based on the batter's height, over home plate that starts at about the batter's knees and goes up to their armpits. A pitch that gets past the batter and is in the **Strike Zone** is a strike. A pitch that goes past the batter and is not in the **Strike Zone** is a ball.

A pitcher who throws their pitch in the **Strike Zone** over the inside or outside edge of home plate is said to **Paint the Corner** or **Paint the Black**. Home plate is white (like the bases) but it is outlined in black so that is where the saying **Paint the Black** comes from.

Framing is a way that a catcher can help the pitcher. When a pitch is close to the **Strike Zone**, but just outside of it, a catcher can quickly move their glove into the **Strike Zone** after catching the pitch, to try to get the umpire to call the pitch a strike.

On The Bump

Toeing The Rubber

Wind Up

Stretch

Pitchers are required to throw from the pitcher's mound while having one of their feet in contact with a rectangular piece of rubber that is installed at the top of the mound. When a pitcher is on the mound they are said to be **On the Bump**. When the player is pitching, they are said to be **Toeing the Rubber**.

When a pitcher is getting ready to throw a pitch, they use either a **Windup** or a **Stretch**. When there are no runners on base, the pitcher is free to use a full **Windup** to create as much velocity (the amount of power and speed) as possible for the pitch. If there is a runner (or runners) on base, the pitcher must keep the runners as close to their bases as possible so the pitcher will use the **Stretch**. For the **Stretch**, the pitcher uses as little motion as possible to throw the pitch, usually just a quick stride forward. If the bases are loaded, then the pitcher has the option of using the **Windup** or the **Stretch**.

Heat

Bullets

Gas

BBs

Cheese

Seeds

When a pitcher throws the ball very fast, they are said to be throwing **Heat**, **Gas**, or **Cheese**.

Pitchers who are throwing the ball very fast are harder for batters to hit and the ball appears to be smaller when it is traveling fast. Batters will refer to the pitcher as throwing **Bullets**, **BBs** or **Seeds** to let other batters know what to expect. The good news for batters is that if they do hit the ball, a fast pitch will usually result in a harder hit.

 Change Up

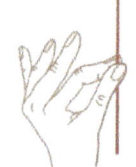 Pulling The String

 Knuckle Ball

Splitter ÷ 2

 Spitball

When a pitcher throws a pitch that is slower than their other pitches, it is called a **Change Up**. The **Change Up** is meant to make the batter think it is a fastball, but it is much slower, and it throws off the batter's timing so that they either miss the ball or hit it poorly. When a pitcher throws a **Change Up** it is also called **Pulling the String**.

Two other "off speed" pitches that a pitcher could throw are the **Knuckle Ball** and **Splitter**. The **Knuckle Ball** is the slowest pitch a pitcher could throw. The pitcher presses their fingertips and/or knuckles against the ball and throws the pitch so that it barely rotates at all. The combination of the slow pitch and lack of spin on the ball increases the air resistance and makes the ball move side-to-side as it travels. The key is for the pitcher to push the ball off their fingers, instead of having backspin on the ball. A **Splitter** is when the pitcher puts the ball between their fingers and throws it like a regular pitch. The pitcher's finger position makes the ball spin much less which makes the ball move like a **Knuckle Ball**, but it is faster.

A **Spitball** is just what it sounds like, and it is illegal. It is when the pitcher puts spit or another substance (like petroleum jelly) on the ball which makes the ball move differently when pitched because the weight and air resistance of the ball have changed. If a pitcher gets caught throwing **Spitballs**, they will be ejected from the game.

Spinner

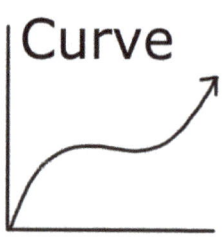
Curve

Hook

Slider

Cutter

Screwball

When a pitcher throws a pitch with sidespin instead of backspin, it makes the ball move differently. The pitches are called **Spinners** and there are different kinds to make the ball do different things.

The most common **Spinner** is a **Curve** ball or **Hook** which the pitcher throws slower to give the ball maximum movement. A **Slider** is a **Curve** ball that is thrown faster than a regular **Curve** ball. It does not curve as much as a regular **Curve** ball, but since it is traveling faster it can fool the batter. A **Cutter** is a very fast **Curve** ball that is thrown almost as fast as a fastball, and it curves at the last second.

A **Spinner** that moves in the opposite direction to the **Curve** ball is called a **Screwball**. A pitcher throws a **Screwball** by turning their wrist inside-to-outside (instead of outside-to-inside for a **Curve** ball) during the pitch, which gives the ball the opposite spin and movement.

When a pitcher throws a **Curve** ball, they are said to **Break One Off**. The term comes from the motion of the pitcher's wrist going through a snapping motion like breaking a piece of chocolate off of a candy bar.

 **Dealing**

 **Great Stuff**

Filthy

When a pitcher has a good variety of pitches and is pitching a strong game they are said to be **Dealing** or having **Great Stuff**.

When a pitcher has **Great Stuff** and they are making the batters look bad, they are said to be **Filthy**.

Submarine Pitcher

Junk Baller

Closer

A **Submarine Pitcher** throws the ball sidearm with a little bit of underhand motion. While most pitchers throw overhand and release the ball at about shoulder height, a **Submarine Pitcher** will release the ball slightly below the height of their hip when throwing a pitch. The spin that comes from the low release point causes the ball to move downward (sink) as it gets to the batter.

When a pitcher throws a lot of different pitches that make the ball move, especially breaking balls such as **Curve** balls, **Screwballs**, and **Knuckle Balls**, they are said to be a **Junk Baller** because they throw lots of junk to the batters.

A **Closer** is a specialty pitcher who comes into the game for the last inning or two, when their team is winning, to finish or close a game and make sure their team wins. **Closer** pitchers are usually very hard throwers and are not afraid to challenge the batters with their power pitches.

Meatball

Gopher Ball

When a pitcher throws a pitch that is easy to hit it is called a **Meatball**. Batters will take advantage of **Meatballs** and get great hits. A **Meatball** is sometimes just referred to as **Meat**.

When a pitcher throws a pitch that is hit over the fence for a home run, it is said that the pitcher threw a **Gopher Ball**.

Brushback

Chin Music

Bean Ball

When a pitcher feels that the batter is standing too close to home plate (crowding the plate) or is digging in for a big hit, the pitcher sometimes will throw a **Brushback** pitch which means that they throw the ball very close to the batter to try to back them away from home plate. When the pitcher throws a **Brushback** pitch up high and near the batter's face, it is called **Chin Music**.

If the pitcher intentionally throws at the batter and hits them, it is called a **Bean Ball**. If a pitcher **Beans** a batter, the batter gets to go to first base and sometimes the pitcher will be warned or ejected from the game.

When there is a runner (or runners) on base, the pitcher can throw the ball to one of the fielders (instead of pitching the ball to the batter) to try to get the runner out if they are off the base. It is called a **Pickoff** if they are able to get the runner out, and an *attempted* **Pickoff** if the runner gets back to the base safely.

When there is a **Full Count** on the batter (3 balls and 2 strikes) the next pitch is referred to as a **Payoff Pitch** because it is going to pay off for either the batter (if ball 4, then the batter gets a walk) or the pitcher (if strike 3, the pitcher gets a strikeout).

Shut Out

No Hitter

Perfect Game

When one team keeps the other team from scoring any runs in a game, the pitcher (or combination of pitchers) is credited with a **Shutout**.

When one team keeps the other team from getting any hits in a game, the pitcher (or combination of pitchers) is credited with a **No Hitter**.

When one team keeps the other team from making it on base, getting any hits or scoring any runs in the game, the pitcher (or combination of pitchers) is credited with a **Perfect Game**.

Fielding

 Pop Up

Fly Ball

 Can of Corn

When a batter hits the ball in the air and it stays around the infield, it is said to be a **Pop Up**. When the ball travels to the outfield in the air it is referred to as a **Fly** or **Fly Ball**. When a **Fly Ball** is hit near an outfielder so they don't have to move very far to catch it, it is called a **Can of Corn** (which comes from saying that the ball is as easy to catch as a can of corn off of a grocery store shelf).

Infield Fly

Infield Fly is a baseball rule that has a specific situation tied to it. The situation is when there are either 0 or 1 out, and there are runners on first base and second base, or first base, second base and third base (bases loaded). With those conditions, if the batter hits a pop fly in fair territory that is able to be fielded by an infielder, the batter is automatically out, and the runners do not have to run to the next base if the ball is dropped. This rule was put in place to protect the runners from a fielder purposely missing the ball to force the runners to go to the next base, in which case, the fielders could get the runners out very easily.

When a pop fly is hit under those conditions, the umpire should yell "**Infield Fly** Rule, the batter is out!" to make sure everyone knows.

Dead Ball

A **Dead Ball** causes the play to stop. If an umpire declares a **Dead Ball**, the play must stop. Base runners do not advance, and fielders stop play. The umpire will instruct the base runners whether they should advance or stay at the base they are on. There are many reasons for a play to stop and a **Dead Ball** to be declared. Examples of reasons for a play being stopped are when an umpire calls time out; a batter is hit by a pitch; a batter hits a foul ball; a base runner is hit by a batted ball; a batted ball bounces over a fence, is stuck in a fence, or rolls under a fence; a thrown ball goes into a **Dugout** or over a fence; or a batted or thrown ball goes into or under an object on the field such as a tarp.

Hot Corner

The third baseman is said to play the **Hot Corner** because most of the time when balls are hit toward the third baseman they are hit hard and get to them very quickly. Usually the third baseman has to make a "reaction" play because the ball is moving so fast, or **Hot**.

When a batter hits a ground ball and an infielder tries to get the ball to make an out, the fielder must move as quickly as possible towards the ball, or **Charge It**, so they can get it as fast as possible. If the fielder does not **Charge It**, it gives the batter or other base runners a better chance to make it to the base safely.

Double Play

Turning Two

Rolling a Pair

Around the Horn

Double Play

Turning Two

Rolling a Pair

Around the Horn

When a batter hits a ground ball and an infielder tries to get the ball to make an out, the fielder must move as quickly as possible towards the ball, or **Charge It**, so they can get it as fast as possible. If the fielder does not **Charge It**, it gives the batter or other base runners a better chance to make it to the base safely.

When the fielders are able to make two outs on one play it is called a **Double Play**. Most often **Double Plays** happen in the infield when there is a runner on first base and the batter hits a ground ball which the infielders catch, then throw the ball to second base and then on to first base. **Double Plays** are also called **Turning Two** and **Rolling a Pair**.

When a **Double Play** happens with the ground ball being hit to the third baseman and they field it, throw it to second baseman and then on to the first baseman, it is said to go **Around the Horn**.

Around the Horn is also used when a batter strikes out (with no runners on base) and the catcher throws the ball to the third baseman, who throws it to the shortstop, who throws it to the second baseman, who throws it back to the third baseman, who throws it to the pitcher.

Bang-Bang Play

A **Bang-Bang Play** happens when a thrown ball hits the fielder's glove very close to the same time that the runner's foot hits the base. Whether the runner is safe or out, the two sounds happening so closely together make it a **Bang-Bang Play**.

Boot

Kick

Through the Wicket

A **Boot** or **Kick** happens when a fielder makes an error by not fielding the ball well and it bounces off their glove. The ball goes **Through the Wicket** when a fielder misses the ball by letting it go through their legs.

Eat It

Handcuffed

A fielder is told to **Eat It** when they have the ball but should not throw it anywhere because they would not be able to get any baserunners out. Rather than throwing it and chancing an error, the fielder just holds the ball.

A fielder gets **Handcuffed** when a batted or thrown ball bounces closely in front of them and they try to catch it but as the ball comes up it hits off the heel of their glove or their wrist and they are not able to catch it.

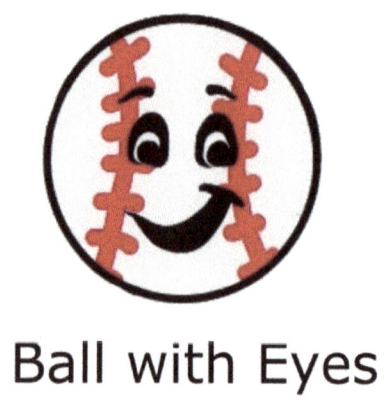

Ball with Eyes

Texas Leaguer

When a batter hits a ground ball that bounces past an infielder for a base hit, it is said to be a **Ball with Eyes** as if it saw the fielder and bounced away from them.

A **Texas Leaguer** is a fly ball that is not well hit that outfielders (and usually an infielder or two) are all trying to catch, but it lands among them for a hit.

When a batter hits a long fly ball and an outfielder needs to make a long run in order to try to catch it, the coach or another player may yell "**Get on Your Horse!**"

Rob

When a fielder makes a great play, like diving to catch a fly ball or line drive, they **Rob** the batter of getting a hit. The most common use of **Rob** is when an outfielder catches a fly ball that is otherwise going over the fence and they **Rob** the batter of a home run.

Throwing Leather At It

Flashing Leather

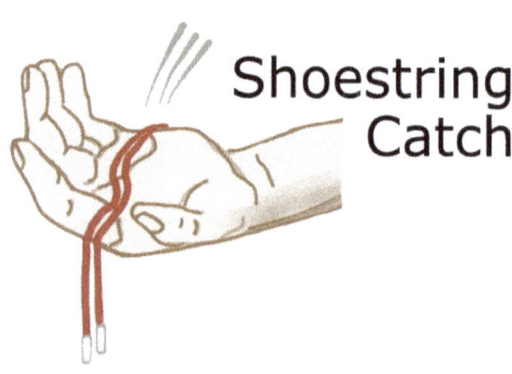
Shoestring Catch

When a fielder makes a great play by stretching, diving or otherwise getting their glove out to make the catch, the fielder is said to be **Throwing Leather at It** or **Flashing Leather**.

A **Shoestring Catch** happens when a fielder, usually an outfielder, runs in to catch a fly ball or line drive and they catch the ball at shoe top (shoestring) level, just before it hits the ground.

Snow Cone

When a fielder catches a fly ball or line drive with the very end of their glove and the ball is sticking out of the end of the glove, it is called a **Snow Cone** catch because the top of the ball and the glove look like a **Snow Cone**.

A **Crow Hop** is a way for a fielder (usually an outfielder) to generate power when throwing the ball. To **Crow Hop,** the player does a running hop in the air with their legs so that when they land, they have more power to throw the ball.

Cannon

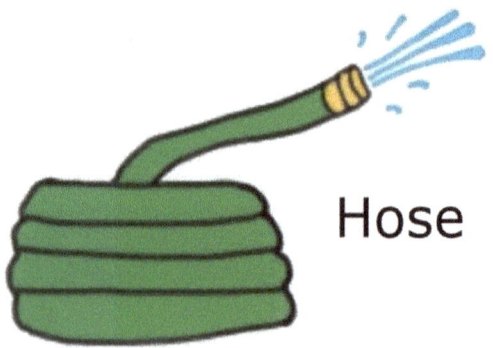

Hose

A fielder with an exceptionally strong throwing arm is said to have a **Cannon** or **Hose**.

Cutoff Man

Relay

When a ball is hit to the outfield and there are runners on base, the outfielder is responsible to throw the ball into the appropriate base. It is the job of one of the infielders to go out to the outfield, between the outfielder and the base where the ball will be thrown and become the **Cutoff Man** for the outfielder to throw the ball to. Once the ball is thrown to the **Cutoff Man**, they then quickly throw it to the appropriate base. This is called a **Relay**.

Pick

When a throw from one fielder to another hits the ground in front of the receiving fielder who catches the ball off the bounce, the player is said to **Pick** the ball. Many times, when players see the situation happening, they will yell "**Pick It**!"

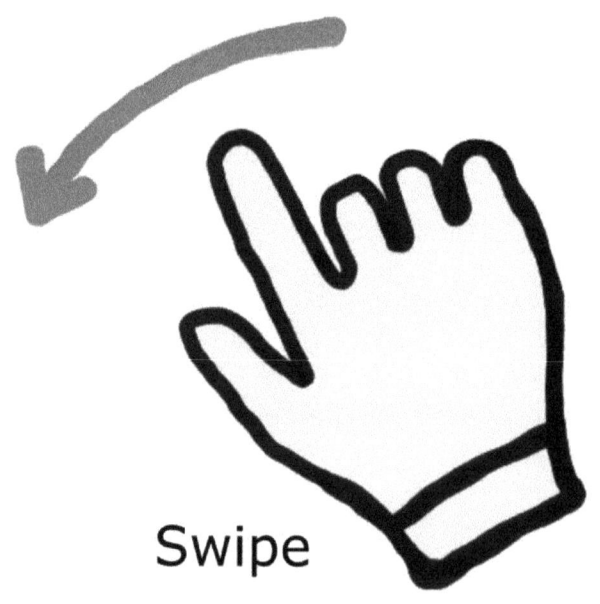

When a fielder has the ball and a runner is sliding into a base, the best way for the fielder to tag the runner out is use a **Swipe** tag. A **Swipe** tag is accomplished by swinging the glove (with the ball in it) in front of the base where the runner is sliding. The fielder uses a sweeping motion and tags the runner's leg (or arm if they are sliding head-first). The sweeping motion is best because it tags the runner and then gets the glove and ball away from the runner so they cannot knock the ball out of the glove.

Index

A
Ahead in the Count, 11
Around the Horn, 119

B
Back to Back, 51
Ball with Eyes, 127
Bang-Bang Play, 121
Base on Balls, 35
Bases Jacked, 53
Batter's Box, 13
Battling, 21
BBs, 85
Bean Ball, 99
Behind in the Count, 11
Bomb, 49
Boot, 123
Break One Off, 91
Brushback, 99
Bullets, 85
Bullpen, 5

C
Can of Corn, 109
Cannon, 139
Caught Looking, 29
Caught Stealing, 73
Change Up, 87
Charge It, 117
Check Swing, 61
Cheese, 85
Chin Music, 99
Choke Up, 23
Clean Up, 15
Closer, 95
Count, 11
Crow Hop, 137
Crush It, 43

Curve ball, 89, 91, 95
Cut, 19
Cutoff Man, 141
Cutter, 89
Cycle, 67

D

Dead Ball, 113
Dealing, 93
Diamond, 3
Dinger, 49
Dish, 13
Donut, 17
Double Play, 119
Down the Pipe, 39
Ducks on the Pond, 53
Dugout, 5, 13, 113

E

Eat It, 125

F

Filthy, 93
Flashing Leather, 133
Fly Ball, 75, 109
Foul Ball, 33
Foul Poles, 7
Framing, 81
Frozen Rope, 45
Full Count, 11, 103

G

Gas, 85
Get on Your Horse, 129
Getting a Piece of It, 33
Give it a Ride, 43
Going Yard, 49
Good Eye, 61
Gopher Ball, 97
Grand Salami, 55
Great Stuff, 93

Green Light, 63
Grounder, 37

H
Hack, 19
Handcuffed, 125
Heat, 85
Hit and Run, 67
Hook, 89
Hose, 139
Hot Box, 77
Hot Corner, 115

I
In the Hole, 13
Infield Fly, 111
Insurance Run, 69

J
Jack, 49
Junk Baller, 95

K
Kick, 123
Knuckle Ball, 87

L
Laser Shot, 45
Laying it Down, 25

M
Meatball, 97
Merry Go Round, 57
Monster Shot, 49
Moon Shot, 49

N
No Hitter, 105

O
On a Platter, 39

On Deck, 13, 17
On the Bump, 83
One Bagger, 41

P

Paint the Black, 81
Paint the Corner, 81
Payoff Pitch, 103
Perfect Game, 105
Pick, 143
Pickle, 77
Pickoff, 101
Plate, 13
Pop Up, 109
Power Alley, 47
Protecting the Plate, 21, 23
Pull Hitter, 59
Pulling the String, 87

R

Relay, 141
Rip It, 43
Rob, 131
Rolling a Pair, 119
Rundown, 77

S

Screwball, 89
Seeds, 85
Shoestring Catch, 133
Shutout, 105
Slider, 89
Snow Cone, 135
Spinner, 89
Spitball, 87
Splitter, 87
Squeeze, 25
Steal, 73
Stepping in the Bucket, 31
Stretch, 83
Strike Zone, 21, 81

Submarine Pitcher, 95
Swipe, 145

T

Tag Up, 75
Tapper, 37
Texas Leaguer, 127
Three Bagger, 41
Through the Wicket, 123
Throwing Leather at It, 133
Toeing the Rubber, 83
Topper, 37
Turning Two, 119
Two Bagger, 41

W

Walk, 35
Walk Off, 65
Warning Track, 7
Wear It, 35
Wheelhouse, 47
Whiff, 27
Windup, 83

Y

Yard, 3